AMAZING DECISIONS

AMAZING DECISIONS

THE ILLUSTRATED GUIDE TO IMPROVING
BUSINESS DEALS AND FAMILY MEALS

DAN ARIELY

ILLUSTRATED BY
MATT R. TROWER

A NOVEL GRAPHIC FROM HILL AND WANG
A DIVISION OF FARRAR, STRAUS AND GIROUX
NEW YORK

Hill and Wang

A division of Farrar, Straus and Giroux

120 Broadway, New York 10271

Text and illustrations copyright © 2019 by The Center for Advanced Hindsight

Printed in the United States of America

Published simultaneously in hardcover and paperback

First edition, 2019

Library of Congress Cataloging-in-Publication Data

Names: Ariely, Dan, author. | Trower, Matt R., author.

Title: Amazing decisions / Dan Ariely and Matt R. Trower.

Description: First Edition. | New York : Hill and Wang, A division of Farrar, Straus and Giroux, [2019]

Identifiers: LCCN 2018044060 | ISBN 9780374103767 (hardcover) | ISBN 9780374536749 (paperback)

Subjects: LCSH: Decision making.

Classification: LCC BF448 .A747 2019 | DDC 153.8/3—dc23

LC record available at https://lccn.loc.gov/2018044060

Our books may be purchased in bulk for promotional, educational, or business use. Please contact your local bookseller
or the Macmillan Corporate and Premium Sales Department at 1-800-221-7945, extension 5442, or by e-mail at
MacmillanSpecialMarkets@macmillan.com.

www.fsgbooks.com

www.twitter.com/fsgbooks • www.facebook.com/fsgbooks

1   3   5   7   9   10   8   6   4   2

CONTENTS

AMAZING DECISIONS

CHAPTER ONE

TWO DIFFERENT WORLDS

DESPITE OUR BEST INTENTIONS, WE OFTEN END UP MAKING BAD DECISIONS. WE OFFEND OUR BEST FRIENDS, STUMBLE THROUGH OUR DATES, AND MAKE DEALS THAT TURN SOUR.

IT'S NOT OUR FAULT – THE UNIVERSE OF HUMAN INTERACTIONS IS COMPLEX.

6

14

16

HOW CAN WE SIMULTANEOUSLY HOLD SEEMINGLY OPPOSITE VALUES? WELL, I'M HERE TO TELL YOU THAT WE ACTUALLY LIVE STRADDLING TWO VERY DIFFERENT WORLDS.

MARKET NORMS RULE ONE WORLD...

...WHILE SOCIAL NORMS RULE THE OTHER.

"NORMS" ARE THE PRINCIPLES THAT GUIDE THE EXPECTED BEHAVIOR IN A GIVEN SITUATION.

LET'S LOOK AT THESE WORLDS ONE AT A TIME...

BEHAVIORAL ECONOMICS RESEARCHERS JAMES HEYMAN AND DAN ARIELY HAVE EXAMINED OUR SENSITIVITY TO SOCIAL AND MARKET NORMS.

WE ASKED PARTICIPANTS TO DRAG A CIRCLE INTO A BOX ON A COMPUTER SCREEN.

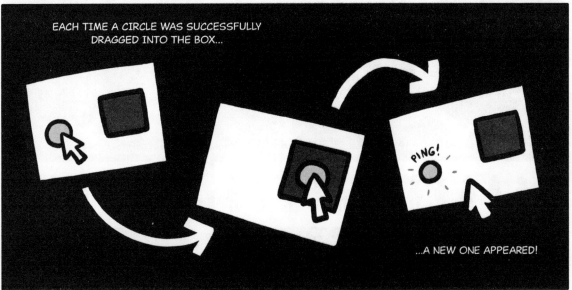

EACH TIME A CIRCLE WAS SUCCESSFULLY DRAGGED INTO THE BOX...

PING!

...A NEW ONE APPEARED!

FOR THREE MINUTES, DRAG AS MANY CIRCLES INTO THE BOX AS YOU CAN. ONCE THE TIME IS UP, YOU CAN LEAVE.

3:00

IT'S AN EASY, IF VERY MONOTONOUS TASK. THE NUMBER OF CIRCLES PARTICIPANTS DRAGGED REPRESENTED HOW MUCH EFFORT THEY WERE WILLING TO PUT INTO THE TASK.

THE PARTICIPANTS IN THE STUDY WERE RANDOMLY DIVIDED INTO THREE DIFFERENT GROUPS.

RESEARCHERS USE RANDOMIZED GROUPS SO THAT ANY DIFFERENCES BETWEEN THE GROUPS ARE DUE TO THE EXPERIMENT AND NOT DUE TO DIFFERENCES BETWEEN THE PARTICIPANTS THEMSELVES...

...THIS WAY, ANY INDIVIDUAL DIFFERENCES AND QUIRKS BALANCE ONE ANOTHER OUT.

(THE LARGER THE GROUPS, THE BETTER.)

RANDOMIZE!

IN AN EXPERIMENT, EACH OF THESE GROUPS IS CALLED A "CONDITION."

OFTEN, ONE OF THE CONDITIONS IS CALLED THE "CONTROL," WHERE NOTHING IS CHANGED AT ALL.

JUST THE BASICS OVER HERE!

IN THIS STUDY, THE CONDITIONS VARIED BY HOW MUCH PARTICIPANTS WERE REWARDED FOR THEIR TIME.

THE STUDY HAD THREE CONDITIONS: A CONTROL CONDITION AND TWO TREATMENT CONDITIONS. IN THE HIGH-PAYMENT CONDITION, PARTICIPANTS WERE GIVEN $4 FOR THEIR WORK BEFORE STARTING THE TASK.

PARTICIPANTS IN THE LOW-PAYMENT CONDITION GOT A SMALLER REWARD OF 10¢ BEFORE STARTING THE TASK.

IN MOST EXPERIMENTS, THIS ONE INCLUDED, PARTICIPANTS KNOW ONLY ABOUT THEIR OWN CONDITION – THEY ARE "BLIND" TO THE REST OF THE EXPERIMENT.

SO, NONE OF THE PARTICIPANTS KNEW ANYTHING ABOUT OTHER PARTICIPANTS OR CONDITIONS.

ASKING THE PARTICIPANTS TO WORK WITHOUT MENTIONING ANYTHING ABOUT PAY SHOWED THE POWER OF SOCIAL NORMS: THAT WE WILL HAPPILY WORK HARD OUT OF GOODWILL ALONE.

AS SOON AS MONEY WAS INTRODUCED, EVEN JUST 10¢, THE TASK BECAME PAID LABOR – AND PEOPLE ADJUSTED THEIR EFFORT ACCORDINGLY.

SO, MIXING THE MARKET AND SOCIAL APPROACHES WON'T NECESSARILY COMBINE THEIR EFFECTS...

...BECAUSE MARKET NORMS CAN CROWD OUT SOCIAL NORMS.

RIGHT!

YOU CAN'T JUST ADD THEM TOGETHER!

$$1 + 1 = 2$$

SOCIAL NORMS + MARKET NORMS ≠ BEST RESULT

36

BACK TO THE PRESENT...

YIKES!

SIGH.

IT DID TURN OUT OKAY – SHE ENDED UP GOING ON A REAL DATE WITH ME THE NEXT WEEK.

AND NOW WE ARE HAPPILY MARRIED!

BUT SINCE THEN, I HAVEN'T BEEN ABLE TO FIGURE OUT WHEN TO TALK MONEY...

...AND WHEN TO LISTEN TO MY HEART OVER MY WALLET.

THAT'S WHEN ALL MY CONFUSION STARTED!

SEE, YOU AND ESTHER FRAMED YOUR EVENING VERY DIFFERENTLY.

IF YOU'D EACH UNDERSTOOD THE OTHER'S PERSPECTIVE, YOU'D HAVE BEEN ABLE TO MAKE BETTER DECISIONS!

WHEN MONEY AND FRIENDS MIX, IT'S EASY FOR ONE PARTY TO COME OUT FEELING HURT.

Hm.

SOMETIMES IT'S BETTER IN THE LONG RUN TO LEND YOUR TIME OR GET A FRIEND DINNER THAN TO HAND THEM CASH.

I WISH SOMEONE HAD TOLD ME THAT BEFORE THE THANKSGIVING-DINNER DEBACLE.

DON'T LOOK AT ME! IT'S NOT MY FAULT HUMANS ARE SO IRRATIONAL.

BUT SOMETIMES YOU CAN'T AVOID BRINGING MONEY INTO THE SOCIAL WORLD, RIGHT?

LET ME EXPLAIN WHY THIS APPROACH WORKS. PSYCHOLOGISTS REFER TO THE EMOTIONAL DISTRESS CAUSED BY SPENDING MONEY AS THE "PAIN OF PAYING."

THIS IS THE UNPLEASANT TWINGE YOU FEEL WHEN SIGNING A CHECK OR PUTTING MONEY IN THE PARKING METER.

OOF, I DEFINITELY KNOW THAT FEELING.

SURPRISINGLY, THE AMOUNT OF PAIN IS NOT VERY RESPONSIVE TO THE AMOUNT OF THE BILL. WE FEEL WORSE AS THE BILL INCREASES, BUT EACH ADDITIONAL DOLLAR PAINS US LESS THAN THE FIRST.

SO, PAYING FOR ONE MEAL HURTS, BUT PAYING FOR TWO MEALS DOESN'T HURT TWICE AS MUCH. THIS IS CALLED "DIMINISHING SENSITIVITY."

MEALS PURCHASED

BACK AT HOME...

SUCCESSFUL ROMANCE: FEWER ECONOMIC EXCHANGES AND MORE EMOTIONAL FULFILLMENT!

LOVE ISN'T A BUSINESS CONTRACT.

BUT...ISN'T MARRIAGE A CONTRACT OF SORTS?

RIGHT. PARTNERS ARE AGREEING NOT ONLY TO LOVE EACH OTHER, BUT OFTEN ALSO TO MANAGE THEIR FINANCES TOGETHER — ALL AT THE SAME TIME!

AND ISN'T THAT WHAT WE'RE SUPPOSED TO AVOID? MIXING LOVE AND MONEY?

SURPRISE!

SOMETIMES IT'S UNAVOIDABLE. BUT THERE ARE WAYS TO APPROACH MAKING "CONTRACTS" THAT KEEP EVERYONE HAPPIER.

THE ROOT OF OUR MOTIVATION WHEN GUIDED BY SOCIAL NORMS OR MARKET NORMS IS VERY DIFFERENT. BUT THERE IS RESEARCH SHOWING THAT ONE CAN PRODUCE BETTER LONG-TERM RESULTS THAN THE OTHER!

WHETHER WE ARE YOUNG OR OLD, THE WAY WE ARE REWARDED FOR GOOD PERFORMANCE WILL AFFECT OUR MOTIVATION TO DO THE SAME THING IN THE FUTURE.

INTRINSIC MOTIVATION IS WANTING TO DO SOMETHING FROM THE HEART – WHETHER IT'S MATH HOMEWORK OR TAKING OUT THE TRASH. AND IT IS EASIEST TO COME BY IN THE REALM OF SOCIAL NORMS.

I WANT TO DO WELL!

I'M HAPPY TO HELP OUT.

EXTRINSIC MOTIVATION, LIKE RECEIVING MONEY FOR GOOD GRADES, OFTEN ONLY WORKS LOCALLY, AND JUST UNTIL THE REWARD IS TAKEN AWAY.

I DON'T CARE ABOUT READING.

SOMEONE ELSE WILL DO IT.

WHILE GIFT GIVING IS A TYPE OF EXCHANGE, GIFTS OBSCURE THE TRANSACTION TAKING PLACE...

...ALLOWING EVERYONE TO FOCUS ON ITS SOCIAL VALUE INSTEAD.

REMEMBER THE CIRCLE-DRAGGING EXPERIMENT FROM JAMES HEYMAN AND DAN ARIELY?

RECALL THAT WHEN GIVEN CASH, PARTICIPANTS ADJUSTED TO PUT IN MORE EFFORT FOR $4 THAN FOR 10¢, BUT THEY WORKED HARDEST OF ALL FOR NO REWARD, THANKS TO SOCIAL NORMS.*

*10¢ → 101 CIRCLES, $4 → 159 CIRCLES, NO REWARD → 168 CIRCLES.

USING THE SAME BORING CIRCLE-DRAGGING TASK, THE RESEARCHERS ALSO TRIED REWARDING PARTICIPANTS WITH EITHER A SMALLER OR A LARGER GIFT OF JELLY BEANS.

FIVE JELLY BEANS

HALF A POUND OF JELLY BEANS

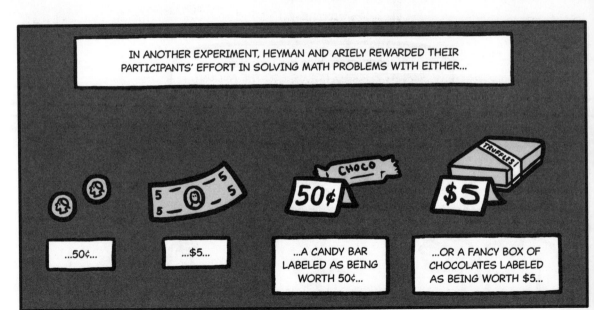

IN ANOTHER EXPERIMENT, HEYMAN AND ARIELY REWARDED THEIR PARTICIPANTS' EFFORT IN SOLVING MATH PROBLEMS WITH EITHER...

...50¢...

...$5...

...A CANDY BAR LABELED AS BEING WORTH 50¢...

...OR A FANCY BOX OF CHOCOLATES LABELED AS BEING WORTH $5...

LIKE SO...

HERE IS YOUR 50¢ CANDY BAR.

HM.

YOU GET A $5 BOX OF CHOCOLATES.

OH!

DO YOU THINK THE CANDY LABELED WITH A DOLLAR VALUE WORKED LIKE MONEY, LIKE A GIFT, OR LIKE SOMETHING IN BETWEEN?

HMMMM

56

IF I REMEMBER CORRECTLY, THE RESEARCHERS FOUND THAT PEOPLE REACTED TO THE EXPLICITLY PRICED CANDY IN THE SAME WAY THEY REACTED TO CASH...

...MEANING THAT THE SMALLER REWARD DEMOTIVATED PARTICIPANTS, LEADING THEM TO PUT IN LESS EFFORT.

THAT'S RIGHT!

THE DOLLAR VALUE CUED PARTICIPANTS TO THINK IN MARKET TERMS.

WAGES EFFORT $$$ OPPORTUNITY COST PAYOFF

IF WE'RE EVEN THINKING ABOUT WORKING FOR MONEY, THEN WE ONLY PUT IN AS MUCH EFFORT AS THE WAGE DESERVES!

50¢

$5

NO MONEY } DIFFERENCE IN EFFORT PREDICTED BY SOCIAL NORMS

MONEY }

50¢ } DIFFERENCE IN EFFORT PREDICTED BY MARKET NORMS

$5

ALL THE GOODWILL THAT THE CANDY GIFTS PROVIDED WAS CROWDED OUT ONCE MONEY WAS INTRODUCED, WHICH ACTIVATED MARKET NORMS.

THAT STUDY SHOWS EXACTLY WHAT YOU DON'T WANT TO HAPPEN WHEN YOU GIVE A GIFT!

RIGHT – A SUCCESSFUL GIFT LIVES IN THE WORLD OF SOCIAL NORMS.

I'M TRYING TO KEEP UP HERE, BUT IT SOUNDS LIKE GIFTS ARE A LOT OF TROUBLE TO GET RIGHT.

WHERE'S THE PAYOFF?

NON-MONETARY GIFTS

I MEAN, I GET THAT MY GIFTEE CAN SPEND A CHECK OR CASH IN A NUMBER OF WAYS...

FOOD

BILLS

FUN

GRAPHIC NOVELS

...BUT MONEY DOESN'T REALLY SHOW ANY EFFORT OR CARING ON MY PART.

EXACTLY! MONEY WON'T NOURISH YOUR SOCIAL BOND WITH THE PERSON RECEIVING YOUR GIFT.

SOCIAL BOND

NOT ONLY DOES IT LACK ADDED EMOTIONAL VALUE, BUT A MONETARY GIFT WILL PRIME MARKET NORMS, AND POTENTIALLY GET YOU IN TROUBLE FOR OFFERING TOO MUCH OR TOO LITTLE.

SOCIAL BOND

A GIFT CARD IS SLIGHTLY LESS EFFICIENT THAN CASH, SINCE IT CAN BE USED ONLY TO BUY CERTAIN THINGS.

NON-MONETARY — GIFT CARD — CASH

BUT DEPENDING ON THE TYPE OF GIFT CARD, IT CAN FEEL MORE LIKE A "REAL" GIFT THAN PLAIN MONEY.

IT CAN SHOW THAT YOU KNOW AND CARE ABOUT WHAT YOUR GIFTEE ENJOYS.

WITH A GIFT CARD, THERE IS ALSO A CHANCE THAT THE RECIPIENT WILL ASSOCIATE ITEMS PURCHASED ON THE CARD WITH THE PERSON WHO GAVE IT TO THEM, TOO.

THERE ARE WAYS TO MAKE THIS EMOTIONAL LINK STRONGER! LIKE CHOOSING A GIFT CARD FROM A SPECIFIC STORE THAT THE RECIPIENT LOVES.

HM...SO A GIFT CARD TO THE DOG-SWEATER BOUTIQUE WOULD HAVE BEEN A BETTER MOTHER'S DAY GIFT FOR MY MOM THAN THE STARBUCKS CARD!

GIFTS ENJOYED THE MOST

- ART
- ELECTRONICS
- EXPERIENCES

- ENTERTAINMENT
- JEWELRY
- OTHER

- CLOTHES
- PREPAID CASH CARD
- GIFT CARD
- CONSUMABLES
- CASH
- HOUSEWARES

POINT IS, EVEN IF THE RECIPIENT ISN'T CRAZY ABOUT A GIFT, ITS PRESENCE WILL STILL PROVIDE LASTING BENEFITS TO YOUR SOCIAL CONNECTION.

THAT SOCIAL BOOST IS WHAT I'D MISS OUT ON BY GIVING ONLY "SAFE" GIFTS OF CONSUMABLES AND MONEY – THEY JUST DON'T DO MUCH TO STRENGTHEN A RELATIONSHIP.

SQUEAK

YES! AND MONETARY GIFTS CAN EVEN DO DAMAGE.

WHEEZE

HOW SO?

WELL, BRINGING MONEY INTO THE EQUATION SHIFTS THE FOCUS TO MARKET NORMS, ERODING THE BASE OF LONG-TERM GIVE-AND-TAKE THAT GOOD SOCIAL RELATIONSHIPS ARE BUILT UPON.

PAY HIM NO MIND...

DEPENDING ON WHERE YOUR INTERESTS LIE...

...A GIFT FROM ANYWHERE ON THE SPECTRUM – FROM CASH TO PREPAID CASH CARDS TO GIFT CARDS TO CONSUMABLES TO JEWELRY AND ART – MIGHT BE RIGHT.

IF YOU DON'T CARE TO BECOME CLOSER TO THE GIFTEE, YOU CAN OPT FOR EFFICIENCY AND GIVE MORE MONETARY GIFTS.

BUT IF YOU'RE INTERESTED IN A SOCIAL RELATIONSHIP, HIDE YOUR WALLET, BECAUSE NON-MONETARY GIFTS ARE WORTH MORE THAN YOU THINK!

THAT SOLVES IT! I'M GOING TO SIGN MY NIECE AND MYSELF UP FOR A POTTERY CLASS! I KNOW SHE'S BEEN DYING TO TAKE A SPIN!

THIS DISTINCTION IS IMPORTANT NOT JUST FOR BOSSES TRYING TO MOTIVATE THEIR EMPLOYEES, BUT ALSO FOR THE WORKERS THEMSELVES.

HUH

WE'D RATHER OUR JOBS BE SOURCES OF FULFILLMENT, RATHER THAN MERELY THE PUNISHMENT WE MUST ENDURE TO GET FOOD ON THE TABLE.

THIS IS ESPECIALLY TRICKY FOR MORE DIFFICULT JOBS.

SANITATION WORKER

SCHOOL-TEACHER

POSTAL WORKER

THE PAY IS FINE, BUT TO BECOME TRULY INSPIRED TO DO A GREAT JOB, I'D NEED TO BE MOTIVATED FROM THE HEART.

HM

OUR SOCIETY DEPENDS ON POSITIONS LIKE SCHOOLTEACHERS AND DMV WORKERS TO FUNCTION.

WHAT IF WE FOUND WAYS TO FURTHER REWARD PUBLIC SERVANTS AND EDUCATORS, SO THEY MIGHT FEEL FULFILLED AND THUS WORK TO THE BEST OF THEIR ABILITY?

YEAH!

HM

IT'S TEMPTING TO TRY TO SOLVE PROBLEMS AT WORK WITH MONETARY INCENTIVES AND PUNISHMENTS...

...BUT AS I'LL EXPLAIN, IT'S ACTUALLY RARE THAT MONEY IS THE BEST SOLUTION, EVEN IN THE WORKPLACE.

THERE ARE MANY OTHER OPTIONS!

GROUP EXPERIENCES...

CLINK

...NON-MONETARY GIFTS...

ADMIT -ONE-

...SOCIAL REWARDS LIKE PUBLIC PRAISE...

EMPLOYEE OF THE MONTH

...AND, OF COURSE, AMPLE BENEFITS.

CONTRIBUTION TO RETIREMENT

HEALTH INSURANCE

SOCIAL NORMS AREN'T JUST USEFUL FOR INCREASING MOTIVATION TO WORK. THEY CAN ALSO GUIDE PEOPLE TOWARD GOOD BEHAVIORS AND AWAY FROM BAD BEHAVIORS. A GREAT EXAMPLE IS A CODE OF CONDUCT.

A CODE OF CONDUCT IS INTENDED TO DISSUADE PEOPLE FROM BENDING THE RULES OR BEING DISHONEST IN BASIC WAYS.

CODE OF CONDUCT

IN 2008, RESEARCHERS NINA MAZAR, ON AMIR, AND DAN ARIELY PUT THE EFFICACY OF CODES OF CONDUCT TO THE TEST.

IN THEIR EXPERIMENT, PARTICIPANTS HAD FOUR MINUTES TO SOLVE A SERIES OF SIMPLE MATH PROBLEMS, EARNING MONEY FOR EACH CORRECT ANSWER.

WHICH 3 NUMBERS ADD TO 10?

		2.91
	1.82	3.05
1.69	4.81	4.28
4.67	5.06	4.57
5.82	5.19	
6.36		

IN THE CONTROL CONDITION, THEIR SCORES WERE TALLIED BY THE EXPERIMENTERS SO THERE WAS NO POSSIBILITY OF CHEATING.

DONE!

MHM

PARTICIPANTS IN ANOTHER CONDITION TALLIED AND REPORTED THEIR SCORES THEMSELVES – MEANING THEY COULD CHEAT TO EARN MORE MONEY BY OVERREPORTING THEIR SCORES.

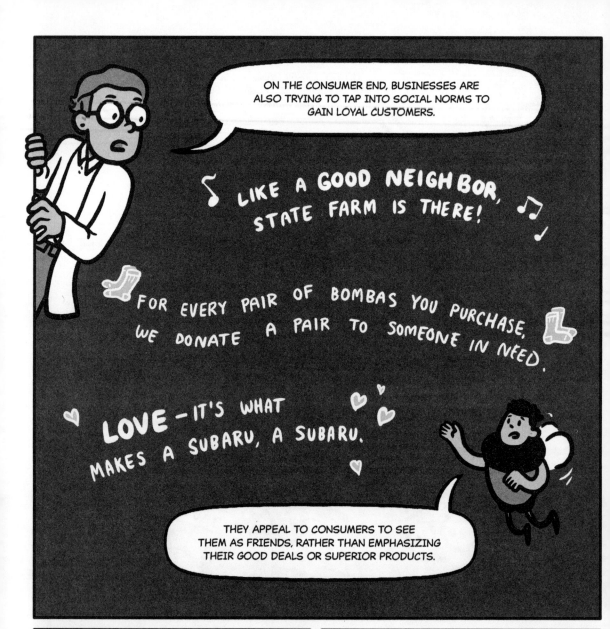

ON THE CONSUMER END, BUSINESSES ARE ALSO TRYING TO TAP INTO SOCIAL NORMS TO GAIN LOYAL CUSTOMERS.

♪ LIKE A GOOD NEIGHBOR, STATE FARM IS THERE! ♪

FOR EVERY PAIR OF BOMBAS YOU PURCHASE, WE DONATE A PAIR TO SOMEONE IN NEED.

LOVE—IT'S WHAT MAKES A SUBARU, A SUBARU.

THEY APPEAL TO CONSUMERS TO SEE THEM AS FRIENDS, RATHER THAN EMPHASIZING THEIR GOOD DEALS OR SUPERIOR PRODUCTS.

BUT BE CAREFUL – THIS STRATEGY CAN BACKFIRE. ONCE CUSTOMERS FEEL BETRAYED BY AN INSTITUTION THEY TRUSTED, THEY WILL ABANDON SHIP...

...AND TELL ALL THEIR PEERS!

IT MIGHT SEEM COMPLEX, BUT WE CAN FIGURE OUT THE BEST STRATEGIES FOR PLAYING WITH SOCIAL AND MARKET NORMS IN THE WORKPLACE.

WHEN FACED WITH THIS KIND OF CHOICE, PEOPLE MIGHT SAY THEY PREFER A MONETARY REWARD...

...BUT DOES IT ACTUALLY LEAD TO BETTER FUTURE OUTCOMES?

THE REWARD-PICKING STUDY HAD A PART TWO (WITH NEW PARTICIPANTS). THESE PARTICIPANTS WERE ASKED TO CONSIDER HOW THEY WOULD FEEL AFTER RECEIVING A BONUS. IN ONE GROUP PARTICIPANTS WERE OFFERED THE MONETARY BONUS, AND IN THE OTHER PARTICPANTS WERE OFFERED THE NON-MONETARY BONUS.

$1,500

LAPTOP
AUDIO SYSTEM
SPORTS TICKETS
TV
CRUISE

ACROSS THE BOARD, PARTICIPANTS IN THE NON-MONETARY CONDITION REPORTED THAT THEY WOULD BE MORE SATISFIED AND ENJOY THEIR REWARD FOR LONGER THAN THOSE IN THE MONETARY CONDITION.

I'D HAVE A BLAST ON THAT CRUISE! I'D ALWAYS REMEMBER IT!

MOTIVATION THAT COMES FROM SOCIAL NORMS CAN IMPROVE A WORKER'S MIND-SET AND LONG-TERM PERFORMANCE.

IN EACH GAME, REACHING A GOOD OR VERY GOOD LEVEL OF PERFORMANCE BROUGHT A REWARD.

BUT POOR PERFORMANCE MEANT NO REWARD AT ALL.

THERE WERE THREE PAYMENT CONDITIONS – LOW, MEDIUM, AND HIGH. THE CONDITIONS VARIED WIDELY IN THEIR LEVEL OF PAYOUT FOR EACH OF THE SIX GAMES.

THE TOP REWARD IN THE LOW-PAYMENT CONDITION WAS 4 RUPEES, THE EQUIVALENT OF POCKET CHANGE...

...WHILE THE TOP REWARD IN THE HIGH-PAYMENT CONDITION WAS 400 RUPEES, THE EQUIVALENT OF A MONTH'S EXPENSES!

AT FIRST GLANCE, YOU MIGHT GUESS THAT PEOPLE WOULD DO THE BEST WITH THE HIGHEST MONETARY MOTIVATION. BUT WHAT DID HAPPEN?

400 RUPEES?!

MHM

AT LOW AND MEDIUM PAY RATES, PERFORMANCE WAS ABOUT THE SAME.

BUT WHEN THE COMPENSATION RATE WAS HIGH, PARTICIPANTS PSYCHED THEMSELVES OUT AND ACTUALLY WORKED MORE SLOWLY AND MADE MORE MISTAKES.

AT A CERTAIN POINT, ADDING MONEY CAN ACTUALLY WORK AGAINST YOU!

LOW

MODERATE

HIGH

IF MONETARY INCENTIVES DAMAGED MOTIVATION AND PERFORMANCE IN THE EXPERIMENT, DO THEY WORK THE SAME WAY IN THE REAL WORLD?

ABSOLUTELY!

UH, WHERE'S THE PROOF?

ONE EXAMPLE IS A REAL-LIFE EXPERIMENT CONDUCTED BY THE GOODYEAR TIRE AND RUBBER COMPANY.

IN 1995, GOODYEAR WANTED TO BOOST SALES OF THEIR LINE OF AQUATRED TIRES.

WE DECIDED TO TEST WHETHER MONETARY INCENTIVES OR TANGIBLE INCENTIVES WERE MORE EFFECTIVE AT MOTIVATING OUR EMPLOYEES.

FIRST, GOODYEAR RANDOMLY SORTED THEIR RETAIL DISTRICTS INTO TWO GROUPS.

FOR THE NEXT SIX MONTHS, SALESPEOPLE IN A MONETARY-INCENTIVES GROUP RECEIVED CASH BONUSES TO MOTIVATE THEIR SALES.

MEANWHILE, SALESPEOPLE IN A TANGIBLE-INCENTIVES GROUP WERE OFFERED A SELECTION OF MERCHANDISE AND TRAVEL-RELATED REWARDS OF EQUAL VALUE.

BOTH GROUPS SHOWED IMPROVEMENT OVER THE SIX-MONTH PERIOD.

HOWEVER, THE GIFT GROUP INCREASED THEIR SALES BY 46% MORE* THAN THE MONEY GROUP!

* 32% INCREASE VERSUS 22% INCREASE IN SALES OF AQUATRED TIRES.

IN 2014, RESEARCHERS LIAD BAREKET-BOJMEL, GUY HOCHMAN, AND DAN ARIELY LOOKED AT HOW DIFFERENT SHORT-TERM BONUSES AFFECTED PRODUCTIVITY IN A COMPUTER CHIP FACTORY.

CHIP CO.

FIRST, THE RESEARCHERS MEASURED EACH WORKER'S BASE LEVEL OF PRODUCTIVITY, MEANING THE AVERAGE NUMBER OF CHIPS THE WORKER COULD ASSEMBLE IN A DAY.

CHIPS: 9

OVER THE NEXT FEW WEEKS THE RESEARCHERS OFFERED THE FACTORY WORKERS A BONUS FOR EXCEEDING THEIR BASE PRODUCTIVITY ON THE FIRST DAY OF THEIR FOUR-DAY WORK CYCLE.

EXCEED YOUR BASE LEVEL ON DAY ONE AND YOU'LL GET A NICE BONUS!

WORK   DAYS OFF

THEY TESTED SEVERAL TYPES OF BONUSES.

CASH

PIZZA-DINNER VOUCHER

FOR YOU

NOTE OF APPRECIATION

WHAT WORKED BEST?

UNSURPRISINGLY, ALL THE REWARDS LED TO INCREASED PERFORMANCE ON THE DAY OF THE BONUS – ABOUT 5% ABOVE WORKERS' BASE PRODUCTIVITY.

5%

BASELINE

BUT, WHEN THE RESEARCHERS LOOKED AT PERFORMANCE FOR THE REST OF THE WORK CYCLE, THE DIFFERENCES BETWEEN SOCIAL AND MARKET MOTIVATION BECAME CLEAR.

WORK   DAYS OFF

WHEN WORKERS RECEIVED THE PIZZA VOUCHER OR NOTE OF APPRECIATION, THEIR PRODUCTIVITY RETURNED TO ITS BASE LEVEL ON THE WORK DAYS FOLLOWING THE BONUS.

FOR YOU

SHRUG   SHRUG

BUT WHEN THEY'D BEEN MOTIVATED BY THE CASH BONUS, WORKERS WERE ACTUALLY 6.5% LESS PRODUCTIVE THAN THEIR BASE LEVEL OVER THE REMAINDER OF THEIR WORK CYCLE!

$ $ $

BLIP BLOOP

IN A 2012 STUDY, RESEARCHERS SEBASTIAN KUBE, MICHEL ANDRÉ MARÉCHAL, AND CLEMENS PUPPE RECRUITED PARTICIPANTS AT A GERMAN UNIVERSITY TO ENTER DATA INTO COMPUTERS OVER THREE HOURS FOR A WAGE OF €12 PER HOUR.

THE CONTROL GROUP RECEIVED THEIR WAGE AND NOTHING ELSE. BUT PARTICIPANTS IN OTHER CONDITIONS WERE OFFERED ADDITIONAL COMPENSATION FOR THEIR WORK BEFORE THEY GOT STARTED:

A €7 BONUS (ABOUT 20% OF THEIR WAGE)...

...A NICELY PACKAGED GIFT OF ABOUT €7 IN VALUE...

OOH

...A CHOICE BETWEEN THE MONEY AND THE GIFT...

HM

...OR €7 FOLDED INTO AN ORIGAMI SHIRT AND PLACED IN A FANCY ENVELOPE.

ALL REWARDS HAD THE SAME MONETARY VALUE, BUT THEY DID NOT GET THE SAME RESULTS.

THE SOCIAL NORM OF RECIPROCITY WORKED FOR ALL REWARDS EXCEPT THE PLAIN CASH.

DEMONSTRATING THAT TIME AND EFFORT WERE PUT INTO THE REWARD ALLOWED PARTICIPANTS TO REMAIN IN THE WORLD OF SOCIAL NORMS, INCREASING THEIR MOTIVATION TO WORK.

BACK AT THE OFFICE...

EVEN IF I DID GIVE YOU MORE MONEY TO MAKE YOU GIVE YOUR BEST EFFORT FOR A WHILE...

...I CAN'T PAY TO MAKE YOU LOVE YOUR WORK AND WANT TO PERFORM BETTER.

THAT'S RIGHT! MY HEARTFELT DEDICATION IS NOT THAT EASY TO BUY!

THIS IS IMPORTANT BECAUSE EVERYONE BENEFITS WHEN EMPLOYEES ARE MOTIVATED INTRINSICALLY INSTEAD OF EXTRINSICALLY.

IN ONE GROUP, EACH CHILD WAS PROMISED A SHINY GOLD SEAL AND RIBBON FOR COMPLETING THE ACTIVITY.

IN ANOTHER GROUP, CHILDREN HEARD NOTHING ABOUT A REWARD BUT WERE SURPRISED AT THE END BY THE SAME SEAL AND RIBBON. IN A THIRD GROUP, THE CHILDREN RECEIVED NO REWARD AT ALL.

WELL, WE'RE DONE.

AFTER THE TEST, VOLUNTEERS RATED THE QUALITY OF ALL DRAWINGS.

Hmm

THE RESEARCHERS CAME BACK THE FOLLOWING WEEK TO MEASURE AGAIN HOW MUCH OF THEIR FREE TIME THE CHILDREN SPENT DRAWING.

THE OUTCOME? THE DRAWINGS BY CHILDREN EXPECTING A REWARD WERE RATED AS SIGNIFICANTLY LOWER QUALITY THAN THOSE MADE BY CHILDREN IN THE OTHER CONDITIONS.

IF THIS SOUNDS TOO WARM AND FUZZY FOR YOU, CONSIDER THIS NEXT STUDY, EXAMINING THE LONG-TERM PERFORMANCE OF CADETS AT WEST POINT, AN ELITE U.S. MILITARY ACADEMY.

RESEARCHERS EXAMINED WHY NEW CADETS WERE MOTIVATED TO ATTEND WEST POINT.

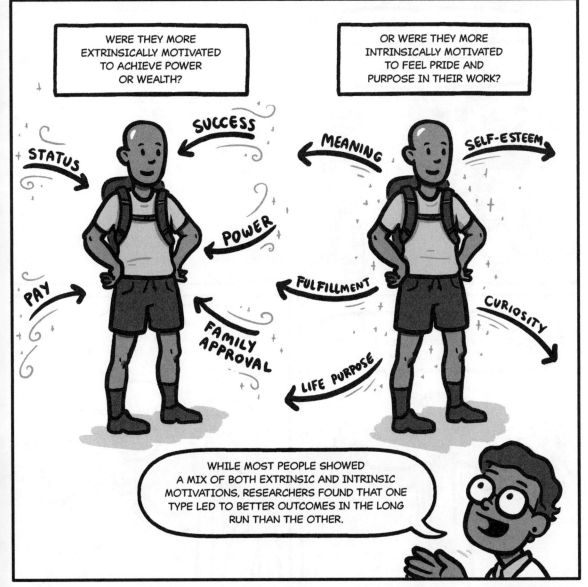

WERE THEY MORE EXTRINSICALLY MOTIVATED TO ACHIEVE POWER OR WEALTH?

OR WERE THEY MORE INTRINSICALLY MOTIVATED TO FEEL PRIDE AND PURPOSE IN THEIR WORK?

SUCCESS

STATUS

POWER

PAY

FAMILY APPROVAL

MEANING

SELF-ESTEEM

FULFILLMENT

CURIOSITY

LIFE PURPOSE

WHILE MOST PEOPLE SHOWED A MIX OF BOTH EXTRINSIC AND INTRINSIC MOTIVATIONS, RESEARCHERS FOUND THAT ONE TYPE LED TO BETTER OUTCOMES IN THE LONG RUN THAN THE OTHER.

OH! SO EMPLOYERS LIKE ME SHOULD TRY TO CREATE GOOD SOCIAL CONDITIONS WHERE PEOPLE ENJOY THEIR WORK.

MANY CORPORATIONS TODAY ARE ATTEMPTING TO FIND A BALANCE IN ORDER TO REAP THE REWARDS OF A MORE SOCIALLY FOCUSED WORK ENVIRONMENT.

GOOGLE IS WELL-KNOWN FOR ITS GENEROUS BENEFITS, INCLUDING FREE HAIRCUTS, GOURMET MEALS, AND "NAP PODS."

ZILLOW WILL PAY FOR EMPLOYEES ON BUSINESS TRIPS TO SHIP THEIR BREAST MILK BACK HOME.

TWITTER OFFERS CATERED MEALS AS WELL AS ON-SITE ACUPUNCTURE TO ITS EMPLOYEES.

BUT NO ONE WANTS TO WORK FOR ONLY GIFTS AND NO MONEY...

IT'S GREAT THAT I HAVE THESE BRANDED HATS AND FREE COFFEE, BUT WHAT ABOUT MY GAS BILL?

AND...

...IF COMPANIES WANT TO HOLD ON TO THE BENEFITS OF SOCIALLY MOTIVATED EMPLOYEES, THEY MUST MAINTAIN THEIR END OF THE SOCIAL BARGAIN.

HUH?

DAY CARE CLOSED (FOREVER)

THEY HAVE TO BE THERE FOR THEIR EMPLOYEES IN HARD TIMES AND DEMONSTRATE THE CARING THAT COMES WITH SOCIAL RELATIONSHIPS.

THAT SOUNDS VERY DIFFICULT. I'M HAPPY TO ADJUST YOUR WORK SCHEDULE.

SNIFF

TO ME, THAT'S JUST COMMON SENSE!

BUT IT'S EASY TO UNDERESTIMATE THE POWER OF SOCIAL NORMS IF YOU'RE FOCUSED ON MONEY ALONE.

CHAPTER SIX

GOING TO THE MARKET
AND BACK AGAIN

WHEN ADDRESSING A MOTIVATIONAL CHALLENGE, WE MAY BE TEMPTED TO DIP IN BOTH POOLS: SOCIAL NORMS AND MARKET NORMS.

BUT IS THERE A RISK IN SWITCHING BACK AND FORTH AS NEEDED? ADAM'S ABOUT TO FIND OUT.

ADAM'S NEIGHBOR JESSE TAKES PRIDE IN HIS HUGE GARDEN.

FOR YEARS, HE HAS OFFERED ADAM A BIG BASKET OF TOMATOES.

HERE YOU GO, BUD!

IT'S A GIFT GIVEN PURELY OUT OF NEIGHBORLY LOVE AND THE JOY OF SHARING ONE'S HANDIWORK.

PREVIOUSLY, ADAM DEMONSTRATED HIS THANKS WITH A SMALL TREAT MADE FROM THE TOMATOES.

tomato sauce ♥

BUT LAST YEAR, ADAM THOUGHT HE HAD A BETTER IDEA.

MAYBE HE IS SICK OF MY TOMATO SAUCE!

WELL, THAT WAS DISAPPOINTING, HUH?

I SHOULD'VE KNOWN NOT TO BRING MONEY INTO IT.

POOF!

POOF!

YOU'LL HAVE A HARD TIME GETTING BACK TO NEIGHBORLY LOVE NOW THAT HE SEES THE TOMATOES AS A BUSINESS TRANSACTION.

BUT CAN YOU REALLY BLAME JESSE FOR SEIZING AN OPPORTUNITY WHEN IT PRESENTS ITSELF?

A 2001 STUDY OF DAY CARES BY URI GNEEZY AND ALDO RUSTICHINI CAN GIVE US SOME CONCRETE ANSWERS.

IN EVERY DAY CARE CENTER, FROM TIME TO TIME, PARENTS ARRIVE LATE TO PICK UP THEIR KIDS.

THIS MEANS THAT THE TEACHERS HAVE TO WAIT AROUND AFTER THE END OF THEIR WORKDAY UNTIL THE PARENTS ARRIVE.

WHILE IN GENERAL THERE ISN'T A SPECIFIC PENALTY FOR LATENESS, THERE IS AN UNSPOKEN SOCIAL CONTRACT SAYING THAT PARENTS GENERALLY TRY TO ARRIVE ON TIME AND FEEL VERY GUILTY WHEN LATE.

I FEEL TERRIBLE. THIS MAKES ME LOOK LIKE A BAD PARENT AND AN INCONSIDERATE PERSON!

IN THIS STUDY, THE RESEARCHERS RANDOMLY SORTED TEN DAY CARES INTO TWO GROUPS. THEY OBSERVED THE BASELINE RATE OF LATE PICKUPS AT DAY CARES IN BOTH GROUPS FOR FOUR WEEKS.

○ CONTROL GROUP
● TREATMENT GROUP

NEXT, THEY DECIDED TO TEST WHETHER IMPOSING A SMALL FINE WAS AN EFFECTIVE DETERRENT TO LATENESS.

IN THE TREATMENT GROUP, THEY INTRODUCED A FINE FOR EVERY TIME PARENTS WERE MORE THAN TEN MINUTES LATE. DAY CARES IN THE CONTROL GROUP HAD NO FINE.

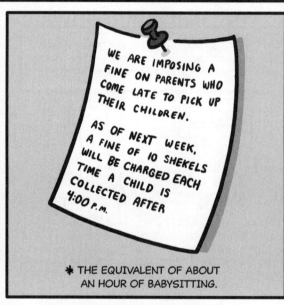

WE ARE IMPOSING A FINE ON PARENTS WHO COME LATE TO PICK UP THEIR CHILDREN.

AS OF NEXT WEEK, A FINE OF 10 SHEKELS WILL BE CHARGED EACH TIME A CHILD IS COLLECTED AFTER 4:00 P.M.

* THE EQUIVALENT OF ABOUT AN HOUR OF BABYSITTING.

SO, DID IT DECREASE THE RATE OF LATENESS?

URI GNEEZY   ALDO RUSTICHINI

JUST THE OPPOSITE! IT BACKFIRED!

FROM THE PARENTS' POINT OF VIEW, BOTH THE SOCIAL PENALTY OF SHAME AND THE MARKET PENALTY OF FINES HAD BEEN REMOVED FROM THE LATENESS EQUATION, SO THEY SHOWED UP LATE MORE FREQUENTLY.

EH, NO RUSH.

SLURRRP

WHAT A MESS!

I CAN KIND OF SEE WHERE THEY WERE COMING FROM, THOUGH.

EVEN A PRICE INCREASE, ROLLED OUT IN THE WRONG WAY, CAN CHANGE THE NATURE OF A RELATIONSHIP. JUST ASK NETFLIX!

FOR YEARS, CUSTOMERS COULD USE BOTH STREAMING AND RENTAL SERVICES FOR $9.99 A MONTH. BUT IN 2011, NETFLIX ANNOUNCED IT WAS SPLITTING UP THE TWO SERVICES AND CHARGING 60% MORE TO USE BOTH SIMULTANEOUSLY.

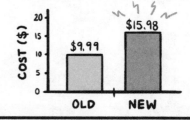

TO CONTINUE STREAMING MOVIES, USERS NEEDED TO BOTH ACCEPT A PRICE BUMP AND CREATE AN ACCOUNT WITH THE STREAMING SERVICE, CALLED QWIKSTER.

CUSTOMERS WHO JUST USED ONE SERVICE DIDN'T MIND MUCH. BUT EVERYONE ELSE WAS UPSET BY WHAT FELT LIKE AN UNFAIR SURPRISE PRICE BUMP AND ANNOYED BY THE PROSPECT OF CREATING A SUPERFLUOUS ACCOUNT.

THIS FELT LIKE A HUGE BETRAYAL TO PREVIOUSLY LOYAL CUSTOMERS.

FOR ALL MY LOYALTY, I'M REWARDED BY HAVING THE RUG PULLED OUT FROM UNDER ME?

THE PERCEIVED UNFAIRNESS OF THIS PRICE INCREASE PROMPTED MANY PREVIOUSLY LOYAL CUSTOMERS TO JUMP SHIP.

SCREW THIS!

IN A MONTH, NETFLIX LOST ABOUT 800,000 OF ITS 12 MILLION SUBSCRIBERS, AND ITS STOCK DROPPED STEEPLY. NETFLIX PROMPTLY APOLOGIZED PROFUSELY AND KEPT DVD AND STREAMING SERVICES TOGETHER AS BEFORE.

2011 NETFLIX STOCK

PRICE HIKE

STOCK VALUE

250
200
150

JAN. FEB. MAR. APR. MAY JUN. JUL. AUG. SEP. OCT.

WHILE NETFLIX EVENTUALLY RECOVERED FROM THIS FAUX PAS, IT WAS A SERIOUS HIT AT THE TIME.

BOTH TRUST AND LOYALTY ARE BENEFITS CONNECTED TO SOCIAL NORMS. ONCE ONE IS GONE, SO IS THE OTHER.

FOR EXAMPLE, STEPHAN MEIER'S STUDY AT THE UNIVERSITY OF ZURICH SHOWED THAT ATTEMPTS TO INCREASE CHARITABLE GIVING BY MATCHING DONATIONS MAY UNDERMINE LONG-TERM GIVING.

AT THIS COLLEGE, EVERY SEMESTER STUDENTS ARE GIVEN THE OPTION TO DONATE TO TWO FUNDS SUPPORTING DISADVANTAGED STUDENTS WHEN FILLING OUT THEIR REGISTRATION FORMS.

THE RESEARCHERS TOOK NOTE OF HOW MUCH STUDENTS DONATED IN THE THREE SEMESTERS BEFORE AND IN THE THREE SEMESTERS AFTER THEIR EXPERIMENTAL INTERVENTION.

THE RESEARCHERS WANTED TO TEST WHETHER OFFERING MATCHING DONATIONS LED TO BETTER OR WORSE RESULTS IN THE LONG RUN.

WHILE THERE WERE TWO CHARITIES TO DONATE TO, IN THE PAST, MOST STUDENTS EITHER DONATED TO BOTH FUNDS OR GAVE NOTHING AT ALL.

STUDENTS WERE RANDOMLY DIVIDED INTO ONE OF THREE CONDITIONS:

ONE CONDITION OFFERED A 25% MATCH FOR FULL DONATIONS...

...ANOTHER CONDITION OFFERED A 50% MATCH...

...AND A CONTROL CONDITION MADE NO MENTION OF MATCHING AT ALL.

BACK TO DAILY LIFE...

OOPS! I GUESS IT'S DINNERTIME!

NORMALLY I'D BE TEMPTED TO REMIND THE KIDS ABOUT THEIR ALLOWANCE SO I COULD GET SOME HELPING HANDS...

...BUT TODAY, I THINK I'M GOING TO TRY SOMETHING DIFFERENT.

HEY, KIDS! WE CAN HAVE A MOVIE NIGHT IF YOU CAN HELP ME GET DINNER READY IN UNDER 30 MINUTES!

HMMMM

MOVIE NIGHT!! WOOOOOOO!

OF COURSE WE DID! WE THOUGHT WE HAD THE PERFECT CONTRACT!

WE THOUGHT WE'D COVERED EVERYTHING!

WHAT TO DO IF SHE NEEDED A PLUMBER...

EEEEP!

...OR IF THERE WAS A BREAK-IN!

...OR IF SHE HAD A GUEST AND HE FELL DOWN THE STAIRS!

AAAAAH!

...OR IF SHE SLIPPED WHILE MOPPING THE FLOOR AND FELL INTO THE LAMP, WHICH KNOCKED THE AC UNIT OUT THE WINDOW!

THESE ASPECTS OF THE BABYSITTING PROCESS ARE EASILY OBSERVABLE AND MEASURABLE.

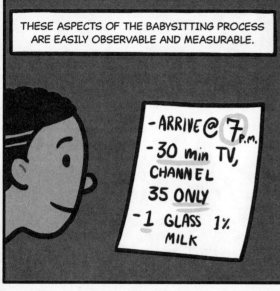

- ARRIVE @ 7 p.m.
- 30 min TV, CHANNEL 35 ONLY
- 1 GLASS 1% MILK

BUT OTHER ASPECTS ARE HARDER TO NAIL DOWN.

- MODEL GREATNESS
- MAKE THEM FEEL CURIOUS
- HAVE A PLAN FOR EVERYTHING

HUH?

EVEN IF WE SPEND HOURS AND HOURS WRITING OUT EVERY RULE WE CAN IMAGINE, WE STILL MIGHT MISS SOME IMPORTANT DETAILS!

LIKE WHAT IF OUR SON STARTS CHOKING AFTER STEALING SOME STALE COOKIES FROM THE PANTRY? SHOULD THE BABYSITTER DO THE HEIMLICH MANEUVER OR CALL 911?

PRETTY OVERWHELMING, RIGHT?

PAT PAT

IN REALITY, IT'S IMPOSSIBLE TO CREATE A 100% COMPLETE CONTRACT.

WHAT?!

IN OUR SOCIAL LIFE, WE MAKE VERY GENERAL AGREEMENTS WITH ONE ANOTHER.

THERE ARE GAPS! THERE ARE GENERALIZATIONS! MANY ASPECTS ARE LEFT UNDEFINED.

WHEN YOU BORROW YOUR NEIGHBOR'S DRILL, FOR EXAMPLE, YOU DON'T FEEL THE NEED TO SPECIFY HOW MANY SCREWS YOU WILL DRIVE IN WITH IT OR TO NEGOTIATE A SUM YOU WILL PAY IF IT GETS DAMAGED.

NEIGHBORLY BOND!

I GUESS WE'D BOTH ASSUME THAT WE COULD WORK OUT ANY PROBLEMS IF AND WHEN THEY ARISE.

WE BASE OUR LIVES AROUND THESE INCOMPLETE CONTRACTS. TAKE MARRIAGE, FOR EXAMPLE!

THE MARRIAGE CONTRACT IS VERY GENERAL.

YOUR DAY-TO-DAY RELATIONSHIP IS NOT REALLY ABOUT DIRECTLY EXCHANGING A FOR B, AS IT WOULD BE IN A COMPLETE CONTRACT.

PICKING HAIR OUT OF THE SHOWER DRAIN

IS NOT OFFERED AS A DIRECT EXCHANGE FOR:

EXPRESSING LOVE WITH A KISS

(FOR EXAMPLE)

BEFORE YOU SAID "FOR BETTER OR FOR WORSE," YOU DIDN'T SIT DOWN AND TRY TO WRITE A LIST OF RULES FOR EVERY POSSIBLE BETTER OR WORSE CIRCUMSTANCE THAT MIGHT ARISE IN THE REST OF YOUR LIVES. THE GENERAL CONTRACT WAS ENOUGH!

IF ONE PERSON GETS SEVERELY INJURED IN AN ACCIDENT AND NEEDS HELP, THE OTHER IS PRETTY UNLIKELY TO SAY, "THIS WASN'T A CLAUSE IN OUR AGREEMENT," AND WALK OUT.

INSTEAD, IDEALLY YOU'D BOTH DISCOVER A WAY TO CONTINUE YOUR LOVING RELATIONSHIP DESPITE THIS UNFORESEEN OBSTACLE, JUST AS YOU'VE DONE MANY TIMES IN THE PAST.

AT ANY GIVEN POINT IN TIME, THERE WILL BE A LEVEL OF INEQUALITY WITH INCOMPLETE CONTRACTS...

...BUT EVERYONE KEEPS AN EYE ON THE GOAL OF LONG-TERM SUCCESS.

TAKING THIS APPROACH TO HEART MIGHT MEAN RECONSIDERING THE BASICS OF HOW YOU AGREE TO MANAGE YOUR RELATIONSHIP

FOR EXAMPLE, DO YOU SHARE YOUR MONEY OR KEEP IT IN SEPARATE ACCOUNTS?

SEPARATE ACCOUNTS

JOINT ACCOUNT

RESEARCH SHOWS THAT MARRIAGES ARE FAR MORE LIKELY TO END IN DIVORCE IF SPOUSES DECLINE TO SHARE THEIR RESOURCES.

AND IT WON'T COME AS A SURPRISE THAT A GENEROUS ATTITUDE IS REPORTED TO BE AN ESSENTIAL CONTRIBUTOR TO A HAPPY MARRIAGE.

DO YOU NEED HELP WITH ANYTHING?

IN EVERY ASPECT OF LIFE, TREATING YOUR PARTNER AS YOUR TEAM MEMBER, INSTEAD OF AS YOUR OPPONENT, IS LIKELY TO PROVIDE BETTER RESULTS.

YOU + ME!

TEAM US

THIS IS WHY IT CAN BE DANGEROUS TO TRY TOO HARD TO COMPLETE A CONTRACT.

HA!!

AS AN EXAMPLE, HERE IS A STORY ABOUT A CAR COMPANY.

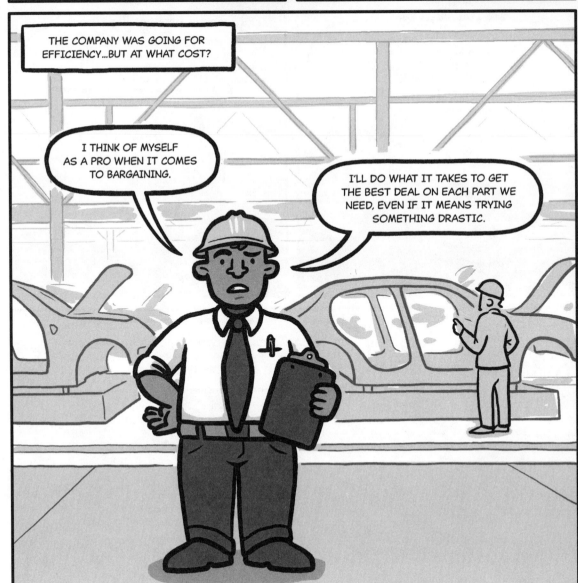

THE COMPANY WAS GOING FOR EFFICIENCY...BUT AT WHAT COST?

I THINK OF MYSELF AS A PRO WHEN IT COMES TO BARGAINING.

I'LL DO WHAT IT TAKES TO GET THE BEST DEAL ON EACH PART WE NEED, EVEN IF IT MEANS TRYING SOMETHING DRASTIC.

THE COMPANY ENDED UP CONDUCTING AN AUCTION WITH ITS PARTS SUPPLIERS TO GET THE LOWEST PRICES FOR EACH SPECIFIC COMPONENT.

ALL RIGHT, WHO CAN GIVE ME THE BEST DEAL ON 129 WHATSIT GENERATORS?

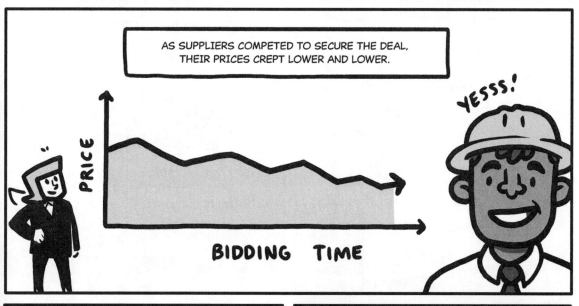

AS SUPPLIERS COMPETED TO SECURE THE DEAL, THEIR PRICES CREPT LOWER AND LOWER.

PRICE

BIDDING TIME

YESSS!

AT THE END OF THIS PROCESS, THE COMPANY DID MANAGE TO SQUEEZE ITS VARIOUS SUPPLIERS FOR THE VERY BEST DEALS ON EVERY SPECIFIC PART.

BUT...

...DOWN THE ROAD, WHEN THE COMPANY FOUND THAT IT NEEDED A FEW PARTS BEYOND ITS CAREFULLY NEGOTIATED ORDERS, IT RAN INTO TROUBLE.

I CAN'T BELIEVE I DIDN'T ORDER ENOUGH WIDGET MOTORS OR FLIP-FLOP DRIVERS!

CAN I GET 100 MORE WITH THAT DISCOUNT WE DISCUSSED?

THE PARTS SUPPLIERS, SEEING AN OPPORTUNITY TO MAKE SOME MONEY, CHARGED THE CAR COMPANY AN ARM AND A LEG FOR EACH EXTRA PART...

UHH...THERE'S ACTUALLY GONNA BE A MARKUP, WALTER.

...INSTEAD OF EXTENDING THE CAR COMPANY THE SAME LOW RATES FROM THEIR INITIAL AGREEMENTS.

HUH?

SINCE THE COMPANY WAS UNABLE TO FORECAST ITS PRECISE NEEDS, ITS ATTEMPT TO CREATE A LINE-BY-LINE AGREEMENT BACKFIRED! IT LOST ITS PARTNERS AND INSTEAD GOT PROFIT-MAXIMIZING SUPPLIERS.

EVEN OUR VERY BEST EFFORTS TO COMPLETE A CONTRACT CAN OFTEN GO ASTRAY.

THAT'S RIGHT!

IT WOULD HAVE BEEN MUCH BETTER FOR THE COMPANY TO DEAL WITH SUPPLIERS WHO UNDERSTOOD THE OCCASIONAL SLIPUP AND WHO WOULD EXTEND THEIR DEALS OUT OF GOODWILL AND THE HOPE OF FUTURE BUSINESS.

SURE, BUDDY. I GOT YOUR BACK.

PHEW

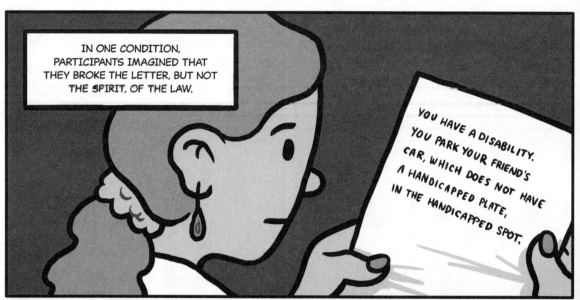

IN ONE CONDITION, PARTICIPANTS IMAGINED THAT THEY BROKE THE LETTER, BUT NOT THE SPIRIT, OF THE LAW.

YOU HAVE A DISABILITY. YOU PARK YOUR FRIEND'S CAR, WHICH DOES NOT HAVE A HANDICAPPED PLATE, IN THE HANDICAPPED SPOT.

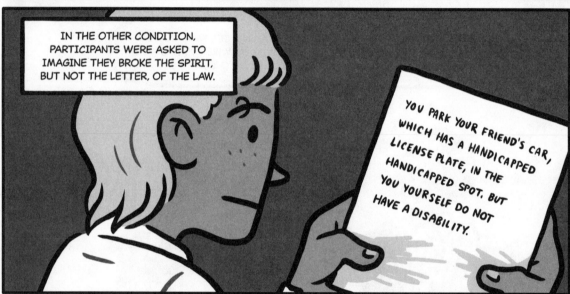

IN THE OTHER CONDITION, PARTICIPANTS WERE ASKED TO IMAGINE THEY BROKE THE SPIRIT, BUT NOT THE LETTER, OF THE LAW.

YOU PARK YOUR FRIEND'S CAR, WHICH HAS A HANDICAPPED LICENSE PLATE, IN THE HANDICAPPED SPOT, BUT YOU YOURSELF DO NOT HAVE A DISABILITY.

NEXT, PARTICIPANTS WERE ASKED THREE THINGS:

DID YOU DO SOMETHING ILLEGAL?

DID YOU VIOLATE THE SPIRIT OF THE LAW?

SHOULD YOU RECEIVE A TICKET?

160

If the letter of the law were king, the results should have looked like this...

CONDITION		
	BROKE LETTER, NOT SPIRIT	BROKE SPIRIT, NOT LETTER
DID YOU DO SOMETHING ILLEGAL?	100% YES	0% YES
DID YOU VIOLATE THE SPIRIT OF THE LAW?	0% YES	100% YES
SHOULD YOU RECEIVE A TICKET?	100% YES	0% YES

*(Vertical label: JUDGMENT)*

...but people actually answered like this.

MPHH

CONDITION		
	BROKE LETTER, NOT SPIRIT	BROKE SPIRIT, NOT LETTER
DID YOU DO SOMETHING ILLEGAL?	83% YES	23% YES
DID YOU VIOLATE THE SPIRIT OF THE LAW?	37% YES	80% YES
SHOULD YOU RECEIVE A TICKET?	57% YES	33% YES

*(Vertical label: JUDGMENT)*

So despite what the law said on paper, about a third of participants cared a lot about whether people were operating in good faith.

These results show that given the option, people care about social norms, even when presented with a seemingly airtight contract, like a parking law.

And if you don't allow people to care about social good?

THAT CAN HAVE CONSEQUENCES! LET ME GIVE YOU AN EXAMPLE.

IN THEIR BOOK *PRACTICAL WISDOM*, BARRY SCHWARTZ AND KENNETH SHARPE INVESTIGATE THE DUTIES OF HOSPITAL JANITORS.

LOOKING AT THEIR JOB DESCRIPTIONS, YOU'LL FIND AN EXHAUSTIVE LIST OF MENIAL TASKS...

YOUR DUTIES
1.
2.
3.
4.

...EVERYTHING FROM EMPTYING WASTEBASKETS IN PATIENTS' ROOMS...

...TO MOPPING HALLWAYS...

...TO REPLENISHING PAPER TOWEL DISPENSERS.

AND YET THIS LONG LIST OF DUTIES IS MISSING SOMETHING VERY IMPORTANT...

...ANY MENTION OF INTERACTING WITH PEOPLE OR USING COMMON SENSE WHEN SOMEONE NEEDS HELP!

MUCH OF A JANITOR'S WORK MIGHT BE MERELY EXECUTING THESE TASKS ONE BY ONE.

MOP FLOORS

CLEAN GLASS DOORS

REPLACE TISSUES

HOWEVER, A GOOD HOSPITAL JANITOR NAVIGATES AN UNPREDICTABLE ENVIRONMENT BY STAYING IN LINE WITH A HOSPITAL'S CENTRAL PURPOSE: TO KEEP PEOPLE HEALTHY, SAFE, AND COMFORTABLE.

FOR EXAMPLE, IF A PATIENT IS DISTRESSED OR IN PAIN, SHOULD THE JANITOR FETCH A NURSE FOR HIM?

OR WHAT ABOUT HELPING A VISITOR FIND THE ROOM OF HER AILING FAMILY MEMBER?

100-175

IN THESE TYPES OF SITUATIONS, WITH A MODICUM OF COMMON SENSE, THE PROPER COURSE OF ACTION IS PRETTY CLEAR.

LET ME FIND THE NURSE FOR YOU!

PHEW

GO THROUGH THE DOUBLE DOORS AND TURN RIGHT!

100-175 →

BUT BY CREATING A DRY, ITEMIZED CONTRACT, THE HOSPITAL WAS ESSENTIALLY DRAWING A CLEAR LINE FOR THE JANITORS BETWEEN WHAT'S "MY JOB" AND WHAT'S "NOT MY JOB."

MY JOB	NOT MY JOB
• MOP FLOORS	EVERYTHING ELSE! (FOR EXAMPLE...)
• CLEAN GLASS DOORS	• HELP LOST VISITORS
• REPLACE TISSUES	• ASK DISTRESSED PATIENTS IF THEY NEED HELP
• WIPE COUNTERS	• SMILE AT CRYING CHILDREN
• TAKE OUT TRASH	• HOLD ELEVATOR DOOR IF SOMEONE IS RUSHING TO CATCH IT
• REPLACE PAPER TOWELS	

IF A JANITOR WAS FOLLOWING ONLY THE LETTER OF THE LAW, IT WOULD BE EASY TO PASS RIGHT BY A VISITOR IN DISTRESS ON THE WAY TO REFILL THE SOAP IN THE BATHROOMS.

THOSE SOAP DISPENSERS WON'T FILL THEMSELVES!

BACK TO OUR DISAPPOINTED HOMEOWNERS...

HM, AFTER HEARING ALL THAT, I THINK I HAVE THE SOLUTION FOR OUR NEXT VACATION.

OH?

CAMPSITE RULE! YOU MUST LEAVE OUR PLACE IN THE SAME CONDITION AS YOU FOUND IT.

PLUS THE BASICS?

PLUS THE BASICS! BUT I WON'T SWEAT THE DETAILS.

AND I'LL REST EASIER KNOWING MY SITTER IS ACTING FROM THE HEART INSTEAD OF ONLY CARING ABOUT THE RULES I PUT ON PAPER.

NOW HE'S GETTING IT!

CHAPTER EIGHT

BIG DEALS

FOR EXAMPLE, ENVIRONMENTAL SUSTAINABILITY IS AN INCREASINGLY URGENT CONCERN. WE'RE USING UP OUR NATURAL RESOURCES!

21 OF 37 OF OUR LARGEST AQUIFERS WORLDWIDE ARE RECEDING, MEANING OUR SUPPLY OF FRESH WATER SHRINKS EVERY DAY.

FURTHER, AIR POLLUTION CAUSES 200,000 EARLY DEATHS IN THE U.S. BUT WE CONTINUE TO FAIL TO MAKE CHOICES TO PROTECT AND CONSERVE OUR WATER AND AIR.

HOW CAN WE START TO CHANGE OUR HABITS AND CONSERVE RESOURCES?

WHY NOT PAY PEOPLE TO POLLUTE LESS?

HIGHER ENERGY PRICES?

FEES FOR TOO MUCH TRASH?

BUT TOO SMALL A PENALTY WON'T CHANGE ANYONE'S BEHAVIOR, WHILE TOO LARGE A PENALTY WILL CAUSE POOR PEOPLE TO SUFFER DISPROPORTIONATELY.

THE MOST POPULAR STRATEGIES MIGHT BE FEES, RULES, AND FINANCIAL INCENTIVES, BUT AMPLE RESEARCH SHOWS THAT HARNESSING SOCIAL MOTIVATION CAN GET BIG RESULTS.

HOTELS ARE CONSTANTLY TRYING TO CURTAIL THEIR USE OF RESOURCES. THEY CAN CUT COSTS AT THE SAME TIME AS THEY REDUCE THEIR ENVIRONMENTAL IMPACT

REDUCE WATER USE

TURN OFF LIGHTS

REDUCE AC USE

STUDIES HAVE INVESTIGATED DIFFERENT WAYS TO GET GUESTS TO REDUCE RESOURCE USE BY DOING ONE SIMPLE THING – HANGING UP THEIR TOWELS INSTEAD OF LEAVING THEM ON THE FLOOR TO BE WASHED AND REPLACED DAILY.

A 2008 STUDY USED DOOR HANGERS TO ASK HOTEL GUESTS TO HANG UP THEIR TOWELS.

SOME GUESTS GOT A MESSAGE ABOUT ENVIRONMENTAL SUSTAINABILITY.

HELP SAVE THE ENVIRONMENT!

YOU CAN SHOW YOUR RESPECT FOR NATURE AND HELP SAVE THE ENVIRONMENT BY REUSING YOUR TOWELS DURING YOUR STAY.

OTHERS GOT A SIMILAR MESSAGE, WHICH ADDED THAT MOST GUESTS HANG UP THEIR TOWELS.

JOIN YOUR FELLOW GUESTS IN HELPING TO SAVE THE ENVIRONMENT! 75% OF GUESTS PARTICIPATE IN OUR RESOURCE-SAVINGS PROGRAM BY USING THEIR TOWELS MORE THAN ONCE.

YOU CAN JOIN YOUR FELLOW GUESTS TO HELP SAVE THE ENVIRONMENT BY REUSING YOUR TOWELS DURING YOUR STAY.

RESULTS SHOWED THAT MORE GUESTS CHOSE TO HANG UP THEIR TOWELS WHEN GIVEN THE MESSAGE ABOUT SOCIAL NORMS.

SHOOP!

% WHO HUNG UP TOWELS

45

44%

40

37.5%

35

30

ENVIRONMENT MESSAGE

ENVIRONMENT AND SOCIAL NORMS MESSAGE

WHEN THINKING IN SOCIAL TERMS, PEOPLE WANT TO FIT IN WITH THEIR PEERS.

I MEAN, EVERYONE'S DOING IT...

BUT WHAT IF YOU WANT TO PUSH PEOPLE BEYOND THE EXISTING SOCIAL NORM?

SOCIAL MOTIVATION CAN STILL HELP!

NOD

A FIELD STUDY BY A DIFFERENT TEAM IN 2012 GAVE HOTEL GUESTS A PIN TO WEAR AND ASKED THEM TO SIGN A CARD COMMITTING TO HANG UP THEIR TOWELS AND REDUCE ENERGY USE.

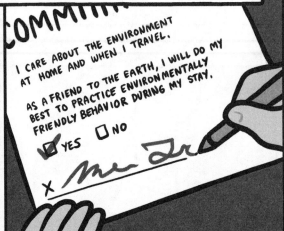

COMMIT...

I CARE ABOUT THE ENVIRONMENT AT HOME AND WHEN I TRAVEL.

AS A FRIEND TO THE EARTH, I WILL DO MY BEST TO PRACTICE ENVIRONMENTALLY FRIENDLY BEHAVIOR DURING MY STAY.

☑ YES ☐ NO

X

ON THEIR OWN, NEITHER OF THESE DEVICES DID MUCH. OF GUESTS WHO RECEIVED ONLY A PIN OR ONLY A COMMITMENT CARD, 60% HUNG UP THEIR TOWELS...ABOUT THE SAME AS GUESTS WHO DIDN'T GET ANYTHING AT ALL.

BUT WHEN GUESTS MADE A SPECIFIC COMMITMENT AND RECEIVED A PIN? 73% OF THEM HUNG UP THEIR TOWELS!

RECIPROCITY FROM GIFT GIVING AND THE NUDGE TO REMEMBER THEIR SOCIAL COMMITMENT TOGETHER PROVED QUITE EFFECTIVE!

THERE ARE MULTIPLE WAYS TO SOLVE A PROBLEM WITH SOCIAL TOOLS. FEEL FREE TO COMBINE – AS LONG AS YOU'RE NOT MIXING SOCIAL NORMS AND MARKET NORMS, OF COURSE!

STIR STIR STIR

WHEN TRYING TO IMPROVE STUDENT AND TEACHER PERFORMANCE, PEOPLE OFTEN DEFAULT TO MONETARY INCENTIVES.

PERFORMANCE BONUSES

FINES FOR POOR PERFORMANCE

PAY FOR GOOD GRADES

WHILE MONEY SEEMS LIKE A TEMPTING METHOD TO CHANGE BEHAVIOR, RESEARCH DOESN'T NECESSARILY SUPPORT THE IDEA THAT MONETARY INCENTIVES RELIABLY LEAD TO REAL CHANGES.

FOR EXAMPLE, A SERIES OF FIELD EXPERIMENTS IN OVER TWO HUNDRED N.Y.C., DALLAS, AND CHICAGO PUBLIC SCHOOLS FOUND THE IMPACT OF FINANCIAL INCENTIVES TO BE "STATISTICALLY ZERO."

IN THESE STUDIES, CHILDREN IN VARIED GRADE LEVELS WERE INCENTIVZED TO READ BOOKS, PERFORM WELL ON MIDTERMS, OR GET GOOD GRADES.

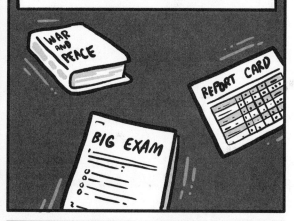

INCENTIVES WERE VERY GENEROUS – MAXING OUT BETWEEN $80 AND $2,000 PER STUDENT. EVEN SO, STUDENTS SHOWED VERY LIMITED IMPROVEMENT OR NO CHANGE AT ALL.

MEH.

BEEP.

IF YOU NEED ANOTHER EXAMPLE, CONSIDER THE NO CHILD LEFT BEHIND (NCLB) ACT OF 2001.

THIS POLICY ATTEMPTED TO IMPROVE EDUCATIONAL OUTCOMES BY INCENTIVIZING SCHOOLS TO ACHIEVE GOOD SCORES ON STANDARDIZED TESTS.

50
45 MPH
1000 MPH

WHILE SOME SCHOOLS MAY HAVE SEEN A BUMP IN TEST RESULTS, RESEARCH SHOWS THAT THE LONG-TERM EFFECTS ON STUDENTS' LIVES WERE GENERALLY NEGATIVE.

BUT...WHY?

FIRST, NCLB USED MONEY TO INCENTIVIZE THE WRONG BEHAVIOR: STANDARDIZED TEST RESULTS INSTEAD OF MORE MEANINGFUL MARKERS OF LEARNING AND SUPPORT.

TEST RESULTS

ENTHUSIASM
CURIOSITY
GRADUATION
ATTENDANCE
SOCIAL SUPPORT
GOING TO COLLEGE
EXTRACURRICULARS

AND SECOND, THE INCENTIVE SYSTEM ACTUALLY UNDERMINED TEACHER MOTIVATION AND THE STUDENTS' INTRINSIC DESIRE TO LEARN AND PERFORM WELL.

FOR MEANINGFUL AND LONG-LASTING CHANGE, IT'S BETTER TO APPROACH THE UNDERLYING ISSUES INSTEAD OF TAKING THE MONETARY SHORTCUT.

EVEN SMALL ADJUSTMENTS TO ENCOURAGE FAMILY INVOLVEMENT CAN BE QUITE EFFECTIVE.

FOR EXAMPLE, RESEARCH SHOWS THAT JUST SENDING BIWEEKLY TEXT MESSAGES TO PARENTS WITH THEIR CHILD'S GRADES AND ASSIGNMENTS CAN IMPROVE PERFORMANCE.

GRADE: B-.

MISSING WORK: 2 PAPERS.

UNSURPRISINGLY, BOTH STUDENTS AND TEACHERS PERFORM BEST WHEN INTRINSICALLY MOTIVATED.

SEARCH FOR MEANING

LOVE OF TEACHING

DESIRE TO IMPROVE

JOY IN A JOB WELL DONE

CURIOSITY

OFFERING TEACHERS CASH INCENTIVES OFTEN HAS NO EFFECT OR ACTUALLY NEGATIVELY AFFECTS PERFORMANCE AND STUDENT OUTCOMES!

HOW IS THAT POSSIBLE?

IN ADDITION TO CROWDING OUT SOCIAL NORMS, MONETARY INCENTIVES CAN BE DISTRIBUTED IN WAYS THAT FEEL UNFAIR.

FOR EXAMPLE...

ONLY TEACHERS IN THE TOP 5% GET A REWARD? I'LL NEVER GET THERE, SO I MAY AS WELL NOT EVEN TRY.

IF YOU CAN'T BUY A TEACHER'S LOVE FOR THE CRAFT OR A KID'S THIRST FOR KNOWLEDGE, WHAT CAN THE WORLD OF SOCIAL NORMS OFFER HERE?

IT COMES DOWN TO MAKING EVERYONE FEEL INVESTED AND SUPPORTED ON A PERSONAL LEVEL: STUDENTS, PARENTS, TEACHERS, AND THE ADMINISTRATION.

ALL THE SAME RULES ABOUT SOCIAL MOTIVATION FOR WORK APPLY TO TEACHERS, BUT TEACHING IS A PARTICULARLY DIFFICULT JOB.

MOST TEACHERS GET INTO THE JOB BECAUSE THEY LOVE (OR AT LEAST LIKE) SHARING KNOWLEDGE – THEIR MAIN MOTIVATION COMES FROM WITHIN.

I STARTED THIS JOB BECAUSE I CARE ABOUT MAKING THE WORLD A BETTER PLACE.

THAT WARM, INTRINSIC MOTIVATION CAN BE KINDLED BY MAKING USE OF SOCIAL NORMS.

PEER MENTORING

FOSTERING COMMUNITY

EMPHASIZING SOCIAL SIMILARITIES

ENCOURAGING INTRINSIC MOTIVATION FOR LEARNING

FOR EXAMPLE, IN THE SOCIAL WORLD, PEOPLE INTUITIVELY CARE FOR PEOPLE SIMILAR TO THEM AND WANT TO DO WELL BY THEM.

A 2015 STUDY OF NINTH-GRADE STUDENTS PUT THIS TO THE TEST. IN THE EXPERIMENTAL CONDITION, RESEARCHERS INFORMED THE STUDENTS AND THEIR TEACHERS OF FIVE TRAITS THEY HAD IN COMMON.

1. SPEAKS FRENCH

2. LOVES THE BEACH

3. PREFERS GROUP ACTIVITIES

4. VALUES HUMOR IN A FRIEND

5. DOESN'T LIKE TO PLAY SPORTS

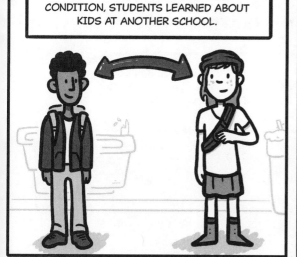

BY CONTRAST, IN THE CONTROL CONDITION, STUDENTS LEARNED ABOUT KIDS AT ANOTHER SCHOOL.

AFTER FIVE WEEKS, STUDENTS IN THE EXPERIMENTAL CONDITION HAD HIGHER GRADES AND PERCEIVED CLOSER RELATIONSHIPS WITH THEIR INSTRUCTORS.

A-

LUCKY FOR US, A STUDY CONDUCTED IN WASHINGTON STATE IN 2006-2008 PUT THIS VERY QUESTION TO THE TEST.

RESEARCHERS TESTED WHETHER INCREASING COMPENSATION FROM THE STANDARD OF $10/DAY TO A MORE COMPELLING $60/DAY* IMPROVED ATTENDANCE.

* APPROXIMATELY MINIMUM WAGE AT THE TIME.

I'VE GOT A HUNCH HOW THIS TURNS OUT...

IF YOU PREDICTED THE EXTRA PAY DIDN'T HELP, YOU'RE RIGHT!

WHEN RESEARCHERS COMPARED RESULTS FROM THE $60 CONDITION TO THE STANDARD $10 RATE, THEY FOUND THAT PEOPLE WERE SLIGHTLY LESS LIKELY TO SHOW UP WHEN OFFERED MORE MONEY.

SERIOUSLY?

THE EXTRA PAY MAY HAVE ENCOURAGED CITIZENS TO SEE JURY DUTY AS A BORING JOB WITH POOR PAY, INSTEAD OF A SOCIAL OBLIGATION.

MEH. I'LL PASS.

THE RESEARCHERS SUGGESTED THAT FOCUSING ON REMOVING CULTURAL BARRIERS TO PARTICIPATION AND EMPHASIZING THE SOCIAL IMPORTANCE OF PARTICIPATION MIGHT PROVE MORE EFFECTIVE.

JOIN US!

WE HAVE AN INTERPRETER!

YOUR COMMUNITY NEEDS YOU!

A FIELD STUDY INVOLVING SCRIPTED PHONE CALLS TO POTENTIAL VOTERS IN NEW JERSEY ILLUSTRATES THIS WELL.

HUFF HUFF

RESEARCHERS PROVIDED VOTERS WITH A MESSAGE REPORTING STATISTICS EITHER ABOUT HOW MANY PEOPLE VOTE IN THEIR STATE, OR ABOUT HOW MANY PEOPLE FAIL TO VOTE IN THEIR STATE.

HIGH VOTER TURNOUT

...OVER THREE AND A HALF MILLION NEW JERSEY CITIZENS VOTED IN THE LAST ELECTION – THE MOST EVER. MANY HOPE THIS TREND WILL CONTINUE IN THE UPCOMING ELECTION...

LOW VOTER TURNOUT

...VOTER TURNOUT WAS THE LOWEST IT HAD BEEN IN OVER 30 YEARS. VOTER TURNOUT IN THAT ELECTION WAS DOWN A FULL 7% FROM THE PREVIOUS GUBERNATORIAL ELECTION...

AFTER HEARING THE MESSAGE, PARTICIPANTS WERE ASKED ABOUT THEIR LIKELIHOOD OF SHOWING UP TO THE POLLS.

THE DIFFERENCE WAS CLEAR: PEOPLE WHO RECEIVED THE HIGH-TURNOUT MESSAGE WERE MORE LIKELY TO REPORT A 100% CHANCE OF VOTING THAN THOSE WHO RECEIVED THE LOW-TURNOUT MESSAGE.

REPORTED 100% CHANCE

80%
75%
70%
65%
60%

HIGH-TURNOUT MESSAGE

LOW-TURNOUT MESSAGE

A LOCALIZED EXPERIMENT IS ONE THING, BUT I DOUBT YOU CAN MAKE SOCIAL NORMS WORK AT A LARGE SCALE.

EASY! USE THE POWER OF THE SOCIAL TIES ALREADY PRESENT IN PEOPLE'S LIVES.

YEP, HE'S TALKING ABOUT FACEBOOK!

LET ME TELL YOU ABOUT A STUDY INVOLVING 61 MILLION FACEBOOK USERS.

61 MILLION!

ON THE DAY OF THE 2010 U.S. CONGRESSIONAL ELECTIONS, RESEARCHERS TESTED THE IMPACT OF EMPHASIZING VOTING AS A SOCIAL EXPERIENCE.

USERS WERE RANDOMLY DIVIDED INTO THREE CONDITIONS.

CONTROL

INFORMATIONAL

SOCIAL

FOR USERS IN THE CONTROL CONDITION, FACEBOOK FUNCTIONED JUST AS IT WOULD ANY OTHER DAY.

STORMIE PURNSLEY 10 MINUTES AGO

J. A. CRAFT 1 HOUR AGO

IN THE INFORMATIONAL CONDITION, USERS SAW THIS POST AT THE TOP OF THEIR FEED.

TODAY IS ELECTION DAY!

VOTE

FIND YOUR POLLING PLACE HERE AND CLICK "I VOTED" TO TELL YOUR FRIENDS.

0115537G FACEBOOK USERS HAVE VOTED!

I VOTED!

THE SOCIAL CONDITION WAS ALMOST IDENTICAL, BUT ADDED PICTURES OF SIX FRIENDS WHO REPORTED HAVING VOTED.

TODAY IS ELECTION DAY!

VOTE

FIND YOUR POLLING PLACE HERE AND CLICK "I VOTED" TO TELL YOUR FRIENDS.

0115537G FACEBOOK USERS HAVE VOTED!

I VOTED!

LISA, JAKE, AND 18 OTHER FRIENDS HAVE VOTED.

RESULTS SHOWED THAT THOSE IN THE SOCIAL CONDITION WERE 2.08% MORE LIKELY TO CLICK "I VOTED" THAN THOSE IN THE INFORMATIONAL CONDITION.

BY EXAMINING VOTER DATA, RESEARCHERS WERE ABLE TO SEE WHICH USERS ACTUALLY VOTED.

THE INFORMATIONAL MESSAGE HAD NO EFFECT ON ACTUAL VOTER TURNOUT, SUGGESTING INFORMATION ALONE WASN'T ENOUGH TO CHANGE BEHAVIOR.

HOWEVER, USERS WHO RECEIVED THE SOCIAL MESSAGE WERE 0.39% MORE LIKELY TO SHOW UP TO VOTE THAN USERS IN THE CONTROL CONDITION.

WHILE THIS MAY SEEM SMALL, TAKING A STEP BACK, YOU CAN SEE THAT JUST THIS TINY ADJUSTMENT CHANGED THE BEHAVIOR OF MANY POTENTIAL VOTERS.

RESEARCHERS ESTIMATED THAT THE EXPERIMENT DIRECTLY GENERATED AN ADDITIONAL 60,000 VOTES – AND 280,000 MORE THROUGH FRIENDS OF FRIENDS VIEWING THE ACTIVITY.

THAT'S 340,000 ADDITIONAL VOTES! ALL FROM A SINGLE FACEBOOK MESSAGE EMPHASIZING THE SOCIAL NORM TO VOTE.

THAT'S INCREDIBLE! I HAD NO IDEA THAT THESE LESSONS ABOUT NORMS WERE SO EASY TO IMPLEMENT AT SCALE!

I KNEW YOU'D COME AROUND.

FOR LARGE CHALLENGES, IT IS OFTEN BEST TO FIRST FIGURE OUT WHICH NORMS ARE MORE LIKELY TO LEAD TO THE DESIRED OUTCOME.

ACROSS THE BOARD, WE HAVE A TENDENCY TO LOOK TO THE MARKET WORLD TO IMPROVE OUTCOMES, WHICH IS WHY IT'S IMPORTANT TO PAUSE AND ASK YOURSELF WHEN SOCIAL NORMS WOULD BE MORE SUITABLE AND EFFECTIVE.

FINANCIAL INCENTIVES CAN WORK FOR TARGETING FINITE, SPECIFIC CHANGES.

CITY PARK

LITTERING IN THIS AREA LEADS TO A $200 FINE!

BUT TOOLS HARNESSING SOCIAL NORMS ARE OFTEN BETTER FOR CHANGING HABITS AND UNDERLYING MOTIVATION.

CITY PARK

IN THIS TOWN, WE TAKE PRIDE IN OUR SPACES. JOIN US IN KEEPING THIS PARK CLEAN BY PICKING UP YOUR TRASH.

IF YOU STAY IN YOUR LANE, I'LL STAY IN MINE.

I CAN AGREE TO THAT!

WE CAN STRATEGICALLY USE SOCIAL NORMS OR MARKET NORMS TO ENCOURAGE PEOPLE TO ACT IN THE BEST INTERESTS OF THEMSELVES, THOSE AROUND THEM, AND THEIR WORLD AS A WHOLE.

WOW! I SURE AM MOTIVATED TO MAKE GREAT CHOICES!

SOMETIMES YOU WILL HAVE TO WORK WITH EXISTING MARKET NORMS IN PLACE...

BUT ALL IT TAKES TO ADD SOME SOCIAL NORMS TO THE MIX IS A LITTLE CREATIVITY AND SOME MINDFULNESS OF THE MOTIVATIONS AT PLAY.

YOU'VE SHOWN ME THAT WE LIVE BETWEEN TWO WORLDS: THE WORLD OF MARKET NORMS AND THE WORLD OF SOCIAL NORMS.

ONE IS CONSTITUTED OF SELF-INTEREST AND COST-BENEFIT ANALYSIS...

...AND THE OTHER OF OUR SOCIAL INTERACTIONS AND RELATIONSHIPS.

AS I DISCOVERED AGAIN AND AGAIN, THE SOCIAL WORLD AND THE MARKET WORLD OFTEN DON'T MIX WELL.

THANKSGIVING

FIRST DATE

TOMATOES

I NOW UNDERSTAND THAT MY SOCIAL WORLD THRIVES BEST IF I KEEP MARKET NORMS AT A DISTANCE!

NOT THAT THERE'S ANYTHING WRONG WITH THE MARKET WORLD – IT JUST DOESN'T FIT WELL WITH MY SOCIAL DEALINGS...AND VICE VERSA.

HMPH!

TRYING TO USE BOTH SOCIAL MOTIVATION AND MARKET MOTIVATION AT THE SAME TIME GOT ME INTO ALL SORTS OF MESSES.

THE TRUTH IS, THEY ARE SIMPLY NOT ADDITIVE.

EACH WORLD HAS ITS OWN SEPARATE ADVANTAGES, COSTS, AND EXPECTATIONS.

$ $ $

USEFUL FOR PRECISE EXCHANGES AND MAKING DEFINITE, SHORT-TERM CHANGES

USEFUL FOR NURTURING RELATIONSHIPS AND MAKING MEANINGFUL, LONG-TERM CHANGES

IT'S IMPORTANT TO BE CONSCIOUS OF WHAT WE WANT TO GET FROM A SITUATION OR RELATIONSHIP...

...BECAUSE THE ACTIONS WE TAKE CAN DRASTICALLY CHANGE THE WAY OTHERS PERCEIVE AND REACT TO A SITUATION.

NOTES

1. TWO DIFFERENT WORLDS

27 *We asked participants to drag a circle*: James Heyman and Dan Ariely, "Effort for Payment: A Tale of Two Markets," *Psychological Science* 15, no. 11 (November 2004): 787–93.

2. GETTING PERSONAL

46 *"pain of paying"*: Dan Ariely, *Predictably Irrational: The Hidden Forces That Shape Our Decisions*, revised and expanded ed. (New York: HarperCollins, 2009).

3. THE GIFT THAT GIVES

54 *the circle-dragging experiment*: James Heyman and Dan Ariely, "Effort for Payment: A Tale of Two Markets," *Psychological Science* 15, no. 11 (November 2004): 787–93.

59 *Cycle of giving*: Lalin Anik, Lara B. Aknin, Michael I. Norton, and Elizabeth W. Dunn, "Feeling Good About Giving: The Benefits (and Costs) of Self-Interested Charitable Behavior," Working Paper 10-012, Harvard Business School, 2009.

66 *how often they gave gifts from different categories*: Guy Hochman, "Gift Giving Survey" (working paper, Duke University, 2013).

4. PUTTING IDEAS TO WORK

79 *In 2008, researchers Nina Mazar, On Amir, and Dan Ariely*: Nina Mazar, On Amir, and Dan Ariely, "The Dishonesty of Honest People: A Theory of Self-Concept Maintenance," *Journal of Marketing Research* 45, no. 4 (December 2008): 633–44.

5. WILLINGNESS TO WORK AND MARKETPLACE MOTIVATION

86 *people generally prefer to receive the money*: Victoria A. Shaffer and Hal R. Arkes, "Preference Reversals in Evaluations of Cash Versus Non-Cash Incentives," *Journal of Economic Psychology* 30, no. 6 (December 2009): 859–72.

91 *In 2009, researchers ran a study in a poor village in India*: Dan Ariely, Uri Gneezy, George Loewenstein, and Nina Mazar, "Large Stakes and Big Mistakes," *Review of Economic Studies* 76, no. 2 (2009): 451–69.

93 *experiment conducted by the Goodyear Tire and Rubber Company*: John M. Jack and Tom K. Gravalos, "The Trouble with Money," *Business Insider Worldwide* (Minneapolis: BI Performance Services, 1995).

96 *looked at how different short-term bonuses affected productivity*: Liad Bareket-Bojmel, Guy Hochman, and Dan Ariely, "It's (Not) All About the Jacksons: Testing Different Types of Short-Term Bonuses in the Field," *Journal of Management* 45, no. 2 (February 2017): 534–54. (Pub. online, 2014.)

99 *recruited participants at a German university to enter data into computers*: Sebastian Kube, Michel André Maréchal, and Clemens Puppe, "The Currency of Reciprocity: Gift Exchange in the Workplace," *American Economic Review* 102, no. 4 (2012): 1644–62.

102 *Intrinsic motivation works from the inside*: Richard M. Ryan and Edward L. Deci, "Self-Determination Theory and the Facilitation of Intrinsic Motivation, Social Development, and Well-Being," *American Psychologist* 55, no. 1 (January 2000): 68–78.

104 *In 1973, Mark Lepper and David Greene conducted a study involving preschoolers drawing pictures*: Mark R. Lepper, David Greene, and Richard E. Nisbett, "Undermining Children's Intrinsic Interest with Extrinsic Reward: A Test of the 'Overjustification' Hypothesis," *Journal of Personality and Social Psychology* 28, no. 1 (1973): 129–37.

6. GOING TO THE MARKET AND BACK AGAIN

123 *A 2001 study of day cares*: Uri Gneezy and Aldo Rustichini, "A Fine Is a Price," *Journal of Legal Studies* 29, no. 1 (January 2000): 1–17.

128 *Just ask Netflix!*: Nick Wingfield and Brian Stelter, "How Netflix Lost 800,000 Members, and Good Will," *New York Times*, October 24, 2011.

131 *Stephan Meier's study at the University of Zurich*: Stephan Meier, "Do Subsidies Increase Charitable Giving in the Long Run? Matching Donations in a Field Experiment," *Journal of the European Economic Association* 5, no. 6 (December 2007): 1203–22.

7. FEELING COMPLETE

145 *At a certain point, the time and effort*: Keith J. Crocker and Kenneth J. Reynolds, "The Efficiency of Incomplete Contracts: An Empirical Analysis of Air Force Engine Procurement," *Rand Journal of Economics* 24, no. 1 (Spring 1993): 126–46.

150 *marriages are far more likely to end in divorce*: Catherine Kenney and Ryan Bogle, "Money, Honey If You Want to Get Along with Me: Money Management and Union Dissolution in Marriage and Cohabitation," Working Paper no. 25, Princeton University, Woodrow Wilson School of Public and International Affairs, Center for Research on Child Wellbeing, May 2010.

150 *a generous attitude is reported to be an essential contributor*: Tara Parker-Pope, "Is Generosity Better Than Sex?" *New York Times*, December 11, 2011, https://archive.nytimes.com/query.nytimes.com/gst/fullpage-9F04E5DA1139F932A25751C1A9679D8B63.html.

159 *A 2014 study led by Stephen M. Garcia*: Stephen M. Garcia, Patricia Chen, and Matthew T. Gordon, "The

Letter Versus the Spirit of the Law: A Lay Perspective on Culpability," *Judgment and Decision Making* 9, no. 5 (September 2014): 479–90.

162 *Barry Schwartz and Kenneth Sharpe investigate the duties of hospital janitors*: Barry Schwartz and Kenneth E. Sharpe, "Practical Wisdom: Aristotle Meets Positive Psychology," *Journal of Happiness Studies* 7, no. 3 (2006): 377–95; Barry Schwartz and Kenneth E. Sharpe, *Practical Wisdom: The Right Way to Do the Right Thing* (New York: Riverhead Books, 2010).

8. BIG DEALS

169 *21 of 37 of our largest aquifers*: Alexandra S. Richey, Brian F. Thomas, Min-Hui Lo, John T. Reager, James S. Famiglietti, Katalyn Voss, Sean Swenson, and Matthew Rodell, "Quantifying Renewable Groundwater Stress with GRACE," *Water Resources Research* 51, no. 7 (2015): 5217–38.

169 *air pollution causes 200,000 early deaths in the U.S.*: Fabio Caiazzo, Akshay Ashok, Ian A. Waitz, Steve H. L. Yim, and Steven R. H. Barrett, "Air Pollution and Early Deaths in the United States, Part I: Quantifying the Impact of Major Sectors in 2005," *Atmospheric Environment* 79 (2013): 198–208.

170 *A 2008 study used door hangers*: Noah J. Goldstein, Robert B. Cialdini, and Vladas Griskevicius, "A Room with a Viewpoint: Using Social Norms to Motivate Environmental Conservation in Hotels," *Journal of Consumer Research* 35, no. 3 (2008): 472–82.

172 *A field study by a different team*: Katie Baca-Motes, Amber Brown, Ayelet Gneezy, Elizabeth A. Keenan, and Leif D. Nelson, "Commitment and Behavior Change: Evidence from the Field," *Journal of Consumer Research* 39, no. 5 (2012): 1070–84.

173 *A company called Opower uses social norms*: Hunt Allcott, "Social Norms and Energy Conservation," *Journal of Public Economics* 95, nos. 9–10 (October 2011): 1082–95.

175 *a series of field experiments in over two hundred N.Y.C., Dallas, and Chicago public schools*: Roland G. Fryer, Jr., "Financial Incentives and Student Achievement: Evidence from Randomized Trials," *Quarterly Journal of Economics* 126, no. 4 (May 2011): 1755–98.

176 *While some schools may have seen a bump in test results*: Marianne Perie and David P. Baker, "Job Satisfaction Among America's Teachers: Effects of Workplace Conditions, Background Characteristics, and Teacher Compensation," Statistical Analysis Report, National Center for Education Statistics, July 1997.

176 *the incentive system actually undermined teacher motivation*: Lisa Guisbond, Monty Neill, and Bob Schaeffer, "NCLB's Lost Decade for Educational Progress: What Can We Learn from This Policy Failure?" *Educação & Sociedade* 33, no. 119 (2012): 405–30.

176 *it's better to approach the underlying issues*: Valerie Strauss, "No Child Left Behind's Test-Based Policies Failed. Will Congress Keep Them Anyway?" *Washington Post*, February 13, 2015.

177 *Just sending biweekly text messages*: Peter Bergman, "Parent-Child Information Frictions and Human Capital Investment: Evidence from a Field Experiment," CESifo Working Paper Series no. 5391, June 24, 2015.

177 *both students and teachers perform best when instrinisically motivated*: Ronald D. Sylvia and Tony Hutchison, "What Makes Ms. Johnson Teach? A Study of Teacher Motivation," *Human Relations* 38, no. 9 (September 1985): 841–56.

179 *informed the students and their teachers of five traits*: Hunter Gehlbach, Maureen E. Brinkworth, Aaron M. King, Laura M. Hsu, Joseph McIntyre, and Todd Rogers, "Creating Birds of Similar Feathers: Leveraging Similarity to Improve Teacher-Student Relationships and Academic Achievement," *Journal of Educational Psychology* 108, no. 3 (2016): 342–52.

181 *some courts report a failure-to-appear rate of up to 50%*: Maxine Bernstein, "Judges Cracking Down on

People Who Snub Jury Duty," Associated Press, May 21, 2017, https://apnews.com/62b279c38615469 fb9bee505c9c66ff5.

182 *people were slightly less likely to show up when offered more money*: Andrew J. Bloeser, Carl McCurley, and Jeffery J. Mondak, "Jury Service as Civic Engagement: Determinants of Jury Summons Compliance," *American Politics Research* 40, no. 2 (2012): 179–204.

183 *in the 2016 U.S. presidential election*: Thom File, *Characteristics of Voters in the Presidential Election of 2016*, United States Census Bureau, September 2018, https://www.census.gov/content/dam/Census/library/publications/2018/demo/P20-582.pdf.

184 *people who received the high-turnout message were more likely to report a 100% chance of voting*: Alan S. Gerber and Todd Rogers, "Descriptive Social Norms and Motivation to Vote: Everybody's Voting and so Should You," *Journal of Politics* 71, no. 1 (2009): 178–91.

186 *users who received the social message*: Robert M. Bond, Christopher J. Fariss, Jason J. Jones, Adam D. I. Kramer, Cameron Marlow, Jaime E. Settle, and James H. Fowler, "A 61-Million-Person Experiment in Social Influence and Political Mobilization," *Nature* 489, no. 7415 (2012): 295.

ACKNOWLEDGMENTS

This book would not be possible without the support of many lab members at the Center for Advanced Hindsight at Duke University. Your insight, humor, and patience bridged all the right gaps. Thank you for joining our grand experiment.

Our gratitude also goes out to everyone who has helped this project come to fruition, especially Jim Levine, Amanda Moon, Laird Gallagher, and Benjamin Rosenstock.

A NOTE ABOUT THE AUTHORS

DAN ARIELY is the James B. Duke Professor of Psychology and Behavioral Economics at Duke University. He is the founder and director of the Center for Advanced Hindsight, cocreator of the film documentary *(Dis)Honesty: The Truth About Lies*, and a three-time *New York Times* bestselling author. His books include *Predictably Irrational*, *The Upside of Irrationality*, *The (Honest) Truth About Dishonesty*, and *Irrationally Yours*.

MATT R. TROWER is a comic artist and illustrator living in Durham, North Carolina. They work as the resident artist for the Center for Advanced Hindsight at Duke University. When they aren't translating research into art, they spend their time petting dogs and zipping up drag queens.